Seven

Essential

Money Skills

*Building a Healthy
Relationship with your Money*

R. Nelson Letshwene

Copyright © 2015, R. N. Letshwene

All rights reserved. No part of this book may be reproduced or transmitted in any form or means, electronic or mechanical without permission from the author and publisher.

Disclaimer:

This publication is designed to provide competent and reliable general information regarding the subject matter covered. However, it is published with the understanding that neither the author nor the publisher are engaged in rendering legal, financial, or other professional advice through this medium. If legal, financial, or other expert assistance is required, the services of a professional should be sought. The author and publisher specifically disclaim any liability that may be incurred from the use or application of the contents of this book.

Published by:

Moedi Publishing

A division of Moedi Learning Technologies (Pty) Ltd;

PO BOX 80927, GABORONE, BOTSWANA

PO BOX 1766 RUSTENBURG, 0323, SOUTH AFRICA

Copyright © 2015, R Nelson Letshwene

CreateSpace Publishing Platform ISBN:

ISBN-13: 978-1512212198

ISBN-10: 1512212199

Moedi Publishing ISBN: 978-0-9870189-4-6

Seven Essential Money Skills™

"With all thy getting, get understanding[1]"

---

[1] Proverbs 4:7

DEDICATION

Dikeledi Mary Letshwene

Makara, Tebogo, Monoshi, Thoko, Marike, Miracle, Serobale, and Moagi

TABLE OF CONTENTS

DEDICATION 4
PREFACE 9
1. Your Relationship With Money 13
2. When We Were Wealthy 19
3. The Seven Essential Money Skills 25
EARNING 31
4. The Sweat Of Your Brow 33
5. Finding Your Skills and Talents 41
SAVINGS 47
6. Why Save Money? 49
7. Make Saving A Habit 55
   Stop Stealing From Your Future Self! 57
   Does Money Slip Through Your Fingers? 59
8. Will You Pay Yourself First? 61
   Goal based Savings 63
   Consider the Power of Compound Interest 65
INVESTMENTS 69
9. Investment Classes 71
   Pension or Retirement Annuity 73
10. Real Estate 77
   The Vacancy Factor 79
   How Do You Calculate Your Rent? 80
11. Sectors of Real Estate 81

1. Residential Sector 81
2. Commercial Sector 84
3. Industrial Sector 85
4. Retail Sector 86
5. Agricultural Sector 86
6. Multi-use Real Estate 87
7. Raw or Undeveloped Land 88

12. The Stock Market 91
Investment Funds 96

13. Entrepreneurship 99

VALUE 107

14. Focus on Creating Value 109

15. Adopt The Farmer's Attitude 115
What is Value? 118
Wire Your Mind To See Value 120

16. The Security Of Owning Your Home 123
Why Should You Own Your Home? 125
Your House Is Not An ATM 125

CONTROL 127

17. What Is Control? 129
Physical Control 130
Emotional Control 132

PROTECTION 135

18. What Is Risk? 137

19. Life insurance And You 141
Why would you need life insurance? 144
Other Insurance Products 147
Legal Entities 148

SHARING 151

20. To Give Or Not To Give 153
Principles Of Giving 154

21. Lending And Borrowing Rules 157
Why Do People Want To Borrow Money From You? 157

EPILOGUE 163

BIBLIOGRAPHY 167

ACKNOWLEDGEMENTS 169

ABOUT THE AUTHOR 171

OTHER BOOKS BY R.NELSON LETSHWENE ...173

PREFACE

"You must get rid of the last vestige of the old idea that there is a Deity whose will it is that you should be poor, or whose purposes may be served by keeping you in poverty"
Wallace D. Wattles

The Seven Essential Money Skills are the most important tools that each person needs in order to build a healthy relationship with money. Most people's involvement with their money starts and ends with an idea called budgeting. But their idea of budgeting is more like fidgeting rather than planning. They would draw what I often call a spending sheet instead of a real budget. It's a spending sheet because it only focuses on the spending side of the money game, with little or no attention given to the earning side. A real budget would obviously give great attention to the income side even before there's a focus on the spending side. Eventually they throw it out, because it doesn't work. It has become a restricting tool instead of a planning tool.

Other people's relationship with money is more like a relationship with other people's money, otherwise known as debt. Debt means other people's money in your pocket.

While budgeting and debt management may be an important part of your relationship with money, they are not even the major parts of the seven essential money skills. They are tiny subsets of the real picture.

The seven money skills are like applications on your smart phone. Until you click on each one of these, they will not reveal to you their true power. You will not know what an app can do until you click on it and explore its functions.

In this book I encourage you to explore these skills beyond what you believe you know about them. They may all look and sound familiar to you, but I encourage you to explore deeply for deeper learning. Great learning happens when you suspend what you believe you know about a subject, and allow it to reveal itself to you in a new way.

Read this book in conjunction with my other book, *The Money Field*[2], for broader understanding of the subject of personal finance. I hope you enjoy your new journey with this book.

Thank you
Nelson Letshwene
November 2015
Gaborone, Botswana

---

[2] *The Money Field – in the game of money, everyone is a player, but some are more skilled than others*, R. Nelson Letshwene, Moedi Publishing, 2015. Also available on www.amazon.com and the digital version in the Kindle store

Chapter 1

1. Your Relationship With Money

"Only the man who has found his true self can know himself, find his own best talents and achieve his own high success."
Napoleon Hill

What is the point of working for forty years to the age of sixty-five and still end up with no money? Asks Bob Proctor, author of *You Were Born Rich*. His answer is that people often run their lives without goals. They conform to the norm and spend their lives seeking to be accepted.

My answer, while in agreement with Proctor about goals, is that people have a dysfunctional relationship with money. Many people do have goals and they often achieve them, but these goals don't include a healthy relationship with money. Professors are people who have set goals to acquire as much education as possible. But professors can also be broke if they don't include among their goals, a functional relationship with money.

Building a healthy relationship with money, in my opinion, starts with mastering the seven essential money skills. In the book, *The Money Field*, I spend time explaining the game of money in which everyone is involved. The book starts with you as a player on the field of play and goes on to tell you about other players who are also interested in your money.

In most cases, we find that other players on the money field are more interested in your money than you are. It is very important to understand the game of money since you are involved in it. This is a compulsory game that everyone who handles money is automatically involved in.

You are naturally opted in by virtue of the fact that you use money. No opting out. You have to play. Getting skilled, therefore, is your only choice.

It is therefore imperative that you incorporate the seven essential money skills in building a functional relationship with your money.

People do work for forty years and end up broke only because they do not seriously get involved in building a working relationship with their money.

Take the skill of saving, for example: Everyone knows about it but many are disconnected from it simply because they misunderstand its purpose in the game of money. Many have tried it in their lives, and yet their lives don't improve. What are the missing ingredients to make it work? We will look deeply into these in the following pages.

People have pension by default, only because their employer deducted their pay to contribute to pension. If they were given their entire money to make their own voluntary contribution, most people would not do it. We know this because most people who work on contracts or are self-employed do not get focused on contributing to their retirement funds.

Most people's relationship with money is focused on consumerism. They think money is something that is there to facilitate consumerism. They consume all they have, and if they run out of their own money, they borrow other people's money to facilitate more consumerism. They then spend the rest of their lives paying off other people's money. At the end of their working life, they are face to face with retirement and they find out that they have not saved enough or acquired enough income producing assets.

Making a decision to build a healthy relationship with your money is imperative in improving your life, both current and your future life. Among all your goals, you should include improving this relationship as a matter of priority.

Too many people have too many negative things to say about money, and that is why they have a dysfunctional relationship with money. They call money evil, problematic, filthy, and all other negative terms. Imagine what kind of a relationship you would have with your spouse or partner if you called them these names. Would they stay? Of course they would leave. And that is why money leaves those who heap insults on it.

When we speak of your relationship with money, we are talking about how you relate to money. Do you have a love-hate relationship, where you love it when it's missing in your life and you hate it when it shows up? That means you long for it when it's not present, but as soon as it shows up you are eager to get rid of it through spending.

Do you see it only as a tool to be used to acquire the things you really want, or do you see that it, on its own account, is also a commodity with which you can build a relationship?

You say you want to be rich, and being rich is measured in terms of money, but you can't keep money long enough to build your riches. How will you reach your goal with such a dysfunctional relationship with money?

It is time to consider how your relationship with money has been and how you can improve it. If and when it improves, you will be eager to learn about investments, about financial protection and prosperity. You will be eager to learn about financial controls and building real value.

The *Seven Essential Money Skills* are your key to building a healthy relationship with your money. Engage each one of them to gain more understanding about the game of money.

Chapter 2

2. When We Were Wealthy

"We consume the bread of poverty because we are hungry, and then it slays us"
Kahlil Gibran.

"The poor you will always have with you", said a very wise man from the plains of Galilee, called Jesus the Nazarene.

Yes we do have poverty of resources, but the greatest poverty is poverty of the mind. Eradicating abject poverty of resources is important, as long as we also eradicate poverty of the mind simultaneously. Why do the poor remain poor? Many arguments can be advanced for this.

Was there a time when we were wealthy? By just examining our life systems of the past, can we find out areas where we were wealthy? How do nations move from poverty to self-sustenance? Let's look at our behaviour as a people during the agricultural age.

When we were wealthy in our minds, we knew not to consume the entire harvest in autumn. We were mindful of the season of winter ahead. We knew not to consume the entire herd or flock. We understood seasons. We could read the times, the clouds, the winds, the droughts, and years of plenty; and this, without complex technology.

When we became poor of mind, we disconnected from our knowingness of wealth systems. What is wealth but a system of self-sustenance? We gave our knowledge and power away to those we elected as leaders and to the industrial complex from which we expected jobs.

When we were wealthy we knew how to invest in our future. We protected our seeds by soiling them with ash to prevent pests from consuming them. We preserved our meat by salting it, drying it, and storing it for the future. We dried our vegetables and preserved them for the future. Even without complex technology, we knew this inherently, and practiced it.

Today, all these practices have been automated, and are therefore forgotten in our minds, since the machines have taken them over. It is now the duty of the commercial system to preserve my food and make my clothes, and the duty of the industrial system to give me a job for the money to purchase my survival.

When we are poor of mind, we consume our harvest without any thought for tomorrow. The planting season is now monthly in the industrial complex called the workplace. Today's harvest is called a salary. It is harvested at the end of every month. Those who have forgotten wealth systems of yesterday consume it without saving any seeds for tomorrow.

We isolated the idea of money from the idea of wealth and we consumed the entire harvest at the end of each harvest season. We made no provision for the future. We set up social security systems. We opened our mouths like baby birds and waited for mama bird to put food in our mouths. Indeed, we eat the bread of poverty because we are hungry, and then, as Kahlil Gibran says, "it slays us". It slays us because we know not where to find it on our own. We are dependents.

When we were wealthy of mind we understood the value of educating our offspring. We let our elders teach wisdom to the young. We taught natural phenomena to our offspring. Ancient tribes like the Basarwa of Kgalagadi whose elders schooled their children around the fire about the behaviour of all animals around them, as well as where to find food and water in the desert.

When we became poor of mind we relegated education to systems. We put our kids in front of televisions and allowed others to influence their minds. We got busy with a dying process called living it up.

When we were wealthy we preserved our culture through meaningful song and dance. When we became poor we let commerce dictate our entertainments. We put aside the harp and the lyre that produced music for the soul, in exchange for meaningless upbeat sounds for the sake of moving the body. And thus the soul has been forgotten.

When we were wealthy we knew the value of everything. When we became poor of mind we knew the price of everything but the value of nothing. We confused price with value, and we lost ourselves in the process. We bought too much house, or too much car, or too much stuff, and forgot to invest in the future of our offspring. They grow up with a silver spoon in their mouth, and know not where the silver comes from. If we do not give up our poverty of mind, what will become of the next generation?

When we were wealthy we knew how to share with each other. Not a one of us went to bed hungry. When we became poor we became traders, and forgot about sharing. If one of us has nothing to trade, they would go home empty handed. The "what's in it for me" mind-set has even penetrated the halls of power and our politicians also thinks this way.

When we were wealthy we never felt insecure. We always felt safe. We did not need protection from each other but we created safety as a collective. When we became poor of mind we became each other's enemies and created rivalries and competitions among ourselves.

When we were wealthy, no job was ever too big for each of us, because we worked as a team. When we became poor we became parasites and some of us stopped contributing and yet continued to demand benefits.

When we were wealthy we had life skills that kept us moving forward in evolution. When we became poor of mind we got caught up in the moment and forgot to reason why we do what we do.

When will we claim our wealth back and give up our poverty?

Chapter 3

3. The Seven Essential Money Skills

"No man can reveal to you aught but that which already lies half asleep in the dawning of your knowledge"
Kahlil Gibran

The Seven Essential Money skills are the building blocks of a healthy relationship with money. It seems that everyone has, at some point heard about one or more of these money skills. The trick is always in the application or implementation process.

Some of these skills are very hard to teach because regardless of how many lectures one can attend, or how many books one can read, the prove of the pudding is always in the eating. If you want to benefit from these skills you have to apply them in your life. Knowing them off by heart may be the beginning, but only their application will bring meaning to your life.

Wiring Your Brain for Success

Have you ever heard of people being "wired" in a particular way? Others call it programming. By constantly thinking in a particular way, your brain gets wired to make that way of thinking your default way of thinking.

When a problem comes, your brain brings up the solutions you have always used in the past for that kind of a problem. If you want a new solution, you will have to think a new thought.

The only way to change your old way of thinking is to get yourself to think differently on just about all subjects. You can only do this if you have taken time to observe yourself. You cannot change yourself unless you know yourself. This requires deliberate and purposeful pursuit.

The "wiring" determines the way you think and the way that you operate. It becomes your second nature. When a particular way of thinking is your second nature, you don't have to strive to think that way anymore. It comes naturally.

Wiring yourself with the seven essential money skills takes practice. The practice may be hard in the beginning, but once you get used to it, it can become a habit.

Think about your own current money habits. What do you "automatically" think of or do when you experience a financial problem? The "automatic" action is your "wiring", your program. If you like your automatic reactions, you're probably on your way to success. If you don't like your automatic reaction to outside stimuli, then you should considered being rewired.

The Wiring of the Poor!

What do you do when you have a financial problem? Many people "automatically" think the only way to solve a financial problem is through a loan. They have not trained themselves to think outside this box. Their lives exist only in this box.

What is your automatic thought process when you come into a large sum of money? Many people's knee jerk reaction is: spending! They do not have an alternative way of dealing with a large sum.

These two examples indicate that these people are wired to get into further financial troubles (loans) or to get rid of money (spending). It is a poverty mindset that will perpetuate poverty.

The Wiring of the Rich!

The financially intelligent are wired differently. They are wired to keep and to grow their money. They are wired to make more and more money. When they have a financial problem, they are wired to solve it without getting into further financial problem. In fact, the solutions they come up with end up creating more and more money for them. So, they really don't mind having financial problems, because it is during the solving of financial problems that they get to make more money.

Let us look at the seven essential money skills and see how each of them is applied on the money field. Could you wire yourself through these skills? Could your new wiring lead you to more success?

This book is only to introduce you to these

concepts and principles. It is your job to find a way to apply them. Application cannot be overemphasized. Let us begin.

The following are the money skills that will be covered in this book.

1. EARNING - Multiple Streams of income through skills, talents and capabilities.

2. SAVING - Purposeful and intentional saving – answering the question *Why?*

3. INVESTING - Understanding Systems for planting Money Trees.

4. VALUE - Time value of money and the value of your performing assets.

5. CONTROL – Emotional control and Physical control of your resources.

6. PROTECTION - Through insurance and legal entities used by wealth builders.

7. SHARING - Frugality and the Abundance mind-set.

1ˢᵗ *Skill*

EARNING

The Capacity for Creative Thought and Creative Increase

Chapter 4

4. The Sweat Of Your Brow

"All work is empty save where there is love, and when you work with love, you bind your self to yourself, and to one another, and to God ... Work is love made visible".
Kahlil Gibran

Everyone is born with some natural talents. Some have more talents than others but just about everyone has natural talents. When we go to school to pursue an education for a career, more often than not, we would like to pursue a career in a field that is aligned with our natural talents. This will give us the greatest capacity for growth and enjoyment in the workplace.

What most people do is, once they have acquired an education that allows them to pursue a particular career path, they tend to forget about all other talents that they have. They focus on this one skill, and this must now support their entire life. This is what gave birth to the "one career for life" mentality of the industrial age.

Yes, the money game does require that you must have a skill you can employ to make money. This may be engineering, medicine, the arts or any career offered by the market place.

There is however, a skill for making and keeping money that may be separate from your vocation. There are people that are skilled in making money, and sadly others are only skilled in spending money. Those who are skilled in making money can spot opportunities for making money from miles away.

They seem to be wired to making money. And they come from all walks of life. Some are educated according to traditional education systems while others are referred to only as street-smarts; they don't have the formal education as defined by our systems of education and yet they are very skilled in the science and art of making money. It is said of these people; whatever they touch turns to gold.

There are others that, no matter how hard they work they never can make enough money. Some people think the ability to make money is a function of how much education you have. So they go out and get as much education as they can afford, and still, they can't seem to be able to make enough money.

Those skilled in making money do not only rely on their school education to sell their skills in the market place. There is a skill of making money that is separate from your professional trade. This is the skill that we are talking about here. A combination of all the essential money skills you will learn in this book, will lead to the building of this skill.

You may be the best astronaut this country has ever seen and still be broke! Being a skilled astronaut, does not necessarily equate to being skilled at making and keeping money.

Having a lot of education does not translate to

your ability to make and keep more money. Obviously, if this were the case, then professors would be the wealthiest people on our planet. But everyone knows, that it is not necessarily so.

The game of money cannot begin unless and until this skill comes into play.

What is earning capacity? It is, quite obviously, the capacity you have to make money.

- Any skill you have that can make you money
- Any talent that can be developed into a money earner
- Any activity that you do that brings you money

The money game begins with your ability to earn money.

How do you enhance your ability to earn money?

1. *By doing more of what brings you money, if it has exponential growth potentials.* Many people are doing more of the same things but these things have no more potential to grow money. This leads

only to fatigue.

In economics we talk of the law of diminishing returns. Increasing effort may increase results to a certain extend, beyond which no amount of effort increased will increase the results. This is knowing that spending two or three more hours on this job will not improve results or perhaps increase your income. Those hours are better off used elsewhere, where there's potential for more growth, productivity, or income.

Exponential growth potential is the key when you pursue the skills that can make you more money. A businessman or entrepreneur is naturally a person who knows how to pursue exponential growth potentials.

Dependence on a salary that only grows at the rate of inflation is tantamount to no growth at all. Exponential growth potential means, with little effort, you can earn results that are far greater than the effort you put in. Pursuing this capacity is one of the most important skills in the game of money.

2. *By continually developing the skills and talents that can earn you money.* In his 1937 book, *Think and Grow Rich*, Napoleon Hill calls it specialised skills. You need to have an arsenal of skills that you can employ to increase your income. Dependence on one skill set may lead you to reach the law of diminishing returns, unless that particular skill set has exponential growth potentials within itself.

3. *By networking with people, in places, doing things, and spending (or rather investing) time on things that can continually improve your life and your earning capacity.* You are not going to grow by wasting your time, your resources, and your relationships.

- *People* are a valuable resource. If you have the right people in your network, you enhance your chances of hearing the right information from the right people so that you can grow. If you hang out with wrong people, you decrease your chances of growth

- *Places* are important too. Certain places have the "wrong energy". Evaluate the places you spend your time and your money in. Do you leave such places inspired or do you leave them depressed?

If your place of work is dull and uninspiring, it will affect you. Perhaps you can liven it up by bringing a plant or some flowers in the room, or put an inspiring painting on the wall. A change of paint or furniture might help too.

• The *things* you do or are involved in will affect your moods and your habits. Some things you own may actually be owning you, because of the controlling power they have on you. Are you a prisoner of your possessions or do you use your possessions for your growth?

• *Time* is a great factor in wealth building. All valuable engagements take time. How you use your time determines whether you succeed or your fail. Lethargy and laziness are big time wasters. Scatterbrain engagements are also a waste of time. This means you are too busy accomplishing nothing, but you can never recover the time you spend on such mindless activities. This includes being a couch potato or mindless charter and activities with friends.

You must avoid people, places, things, and events that waste your time and resources. When you have "nothing to do", you could use that time to work on growing one of your skills or talents. There is no such thing as "nothing to do" – you are always committed to something – even if it's to laziness.

The financially intelligent always employ their skills to make more money.

Your capacity for creative increase starts with your capacity for creative thinking.

Chapter 5

5. Finding Your Skills and Talents

"Every living thing must continually seek for the enlargement of its life, because life, in the mere act of living, must increase itself"
Wallace D. Wattles

The buried treasure within you is your unemployed skills and talents. Any skill and talent you have that is not currently making you money, is a hidden treasure.

In the book, *The Money Field*, I have gone into some detail in helping you to make a list of your skills and talents and to market them to various customers. I will not be repeating that here. In brief, however, here are some steps you need to take to identify your hidden treasures in the form of unemployed skills and talents.

1. Make a list of every skill and talent that you have.

2. Identify those skills and talents that are currently being employed to bring money to you.

3. Figure out how you can expand these skill sets to help you bring more money into your money field

   a. If you are a writer for one magazine, can you write for more or expand to other media like newspapers and online magazines? Can you write a book?

   b. If you are a cook, can you add baking to your skill set? Can you teach others to cook or bake?

   c. If you are an accountant can you start a bookkeeping business? Can you coach non-finance managers?

Every profession has sub-skills that can be employed separately. Can you identify the sub-skills that make up your profession?

4. Write down and look at all the skills and talents that you have that you have never employed to bring you money. Some of the skills may not be related to

your chosen profession at all. But it doesn't mean they just need to sit there doing nothing. They may be needed in industries other than your primary industry of operation. If you are a professional engineer, but you are skilled in fashion design, who is to say you can't pursue those skills and talents as well?

5. Find a way to develop or immediately employ these skills to bring you more money.

The idea of "leaving money on the table" applies to all people with extra skills that could bring them money, but don't employ those extra skills. They just leave that money on the table, so to speak.

Are you leaving money on the table? Have you seen people making money in fields in which you know for certain that you could do even better? What's stopping you from collecting that money?

The development of your earning capacity is the beginning of the money game. This is the primary money skill that gets you going. The process of "wiring" your mind to be a moneymaker starts with a deliberate effort of identifying these potentials and pursuing them.

Now, the development of an additional skill or

talent for the sake of increasing your income will invariably require time, and perhaps some resources. As far as time is concerned, we are all blessed on our planet because everyone, regardless of position in life, gets a full 24 hours per day. Rich or poor, wise or foolish, everyone gets a full 24 hours per day. No favouritism. It is within these 24 hours that we get richer or poorer, we succeed or fail, we do something or we don't do anything.

There is therefore no point complaining that you don't have time. The fact is you have it. You allocate your time to the things you want the most.

When developing an additional skill or talent for the sake of increasing your income becomes important to you, you will allocate time to it.

Find a way to employ your time to your own enrichment. Don't make excuses. Excuses will neither make you rich nor help you reach your goals.

Let me give you a little example in my own life. I have thus far written and published five books. People often ask me where I get the time to do it. I don't claim to be any busier than anybody else, nor do I have less work than anybody else. But here is a habit I created over twelve years ago. I decided to write a minimum of 600 words per week, and I have done that over the past twelve to thirteen years. Six hundred words is not a lot of writing. In fact on average it takes me about an hour to do that. That is just one hour per week.

But because my writing has always been focused on the big picture, this is where all the books that I have written come from.

I did not have to sit down and block out a huge amount of time in order to write the books I have written. One hour per week towards my greater goal has allowed me to have time for many other things that I want.

When you get serious and get focused on developing that additional skill or talent, you will stop making excuses and allocate time to it.

2nd *Skill*

SAVINGS

The Pay Yourself First Principle

Chapter 6

6. Why Save Money?

"The best time to plant a tree is twenty years ago. The next best time is now!"

Chinese proverb

People without a purpose for saving do not save money. And people without a purpose have no time pressure to save anything. If, however, you set up an objective, or purpose for saving, there will be a time horizon as well.

The best time to start saving is now! To wait for just that right time when you think you can afford to save, is to wait for a tomorrow that never comes! If you are not careful you will never start. The key is in knowing your reason to save and when to start your saving.

What is the best motivation for saving money?

No one can answer that question for any other person. The answer is personal. Let us, however, consider the most basic reason for needing to save money. Financial advisors often say you need to have a certain amount of your monthly earnings saved up. The figure often used is six months. The question is why would you want to keep six months of your salary saved up?

That can be answered by another question: If you lost your job today, how long will it take you to get another job? Most financial advisors have assumed the six months period. However, as you know, that number will depend on the economy in which you operate. If in your economy it will take you longer, then you need to adjust that time horizon.

In his book, *Look Within or Do Without*, Tom Bay quotes a Harvard study that shows that even sixty per cent of Harvard graduate live pay-cheque to pay-cheque.

Pay-cheque to pay-cheque existence is very

dangerous, especially if you are still building your life. For most people, their home loan, car payments, school fees for their children, and many other expenses are dependent on this month's salary. If that cheque would not come in because they lost a job, their lives would fall apart. They would lose their house, their car, and their other assets that are still being paid by the salary.

The reason for the six months savings is to make sure that if you should lose your job, while you are still job-hunting, there will be money to service the mortgage, the car loan, and all other expenses.

People who don't have these savings are one month away from disaster! It will take just one month, for your life to fall apart. This is dangerous living.

If you should want just one motivation, then you should save so that in case of such an emergency as losing your source of income, you don't lose your life as well.

How long will it take you to save up to six months of your monthly salary? It may take you years. So the best time to start is now. I meet a lot of people who argue for their expensive living styles while they have no savings at all. They argue that they can't control themselves at the mall and feel compelled to spend their money. And yet they have given no thought to the possibility of losing the source of the income that makes that life style possible. It would make more sense if they already have their six months worth of savings set aside to want to splash out at the mall. But to spend your very last penny and then to wait painfully for the month to end so that you can repeat your lavish lifestyle seems foolish to me. There may be other reasons or motivation, depending where you're at in life.

According to a study of savers by Peter Lunt and Sonia Livingstone published in the Journal of Economic Psychology:

> • "Those who kept their savings rather than using them to pay debts ... had a greater feeling of control over their circumstances,"
>
> • "Similarly, those who save up out of their income at the same time as paying off debts (rather, say, than paying off their debts faster) felt

more in control of their finances and more optimistic about their future than those who did or could not save while having debts."

Knowing that you are in control may be a good motivation for you. People who feel out of control may do things that send them even more out of control. Make sure that you take the controls of your finances.

Another motivator may be, in the words of George Clason, author of *The Richest Man in Babylon*, to "make of your home a profitable dwelling". Clason explains that the first level of focus must always be to own your home. The security that comes with owning your home allows you to play the rest of the money game with ease. But, if everything of yours is still mortgaged to bankers, you are always afraid that you could lose them.

Watch out, you can talk about saving money, but your actions may communicate spending and borrowing. Let's start saving and be in control.

Chapter 7

7. Make Saving A Habit

"Whatever you habitually think yourself to be, that you are ... It is the habitual, not the periodical thought that decides your destiny."
Wallace D. Wattles

The real purpose of saving should be to build wealth. This will happen when you understand investment systems, which we will talk about in the next few chapters. But investments will not happen without a seed from your savings habit.

We all have certain habits that formulate our characters. People who know you often refer to you based on the habits they've seen you do. What you need to do is examine your money habits.

Do you habitually spend money every time it comes into your field? What is the first money habit that you practice when money comes to you?

Your saving will not happen regularly if it's not a habit. Make a habit of saving money. Every time you receive some money, make it a habit of saving a portion of it. Set aside a percentage that you stick to.

Many people are in the habit of attending to emergencies first and foremost. Some are in the habit of consuming money.

Emergencies consume money; they don't build wealth. Certain projects just consume money; they don't build wealth. The primary purpose of saving must be to build wealth. Wealth means a system that you can depend on for more income. It does take discipline to save money. But more than discipline, it takes purpose. Yes, you can save for things that consume money like emergencies, car repairs, furniture, house maintenance, medical emergencies, etc. Categorize your savings and allocate an amount to each category.

- *Saving for family projects:* this can be birthdays, baby showers, bridal showers, holidays etc.
- *Personal Projects* may be if you want to put yourself through school, it can be thought about earlier and saved for.

- *Asset growth* includes saving to buy or build a house, or start a business etc.

In his book, *The Richest Man in Babylon*, George Clason said it best: *"a part of all I earn is mine to keep"*. The principle of keeping money has been at the root of building wealth since money was invented. It is only those that are in the habit of keeping money that can build wealth. It does not matter how much you make, it matters how much you habitually keep.

Those that are expert money spenders do not have a hope of building wealth. The worst are those who play the money game with other people's money, that is, borrowed money.

Stop Stealing From Your Future Self!

When a habit is strong enough, it starts creating other sub habits to support the main one. If you are in the habit of spending your own money, when you run out of your own money, it is very easy to borrow other people's money so that you can keep spending. In this case, the spending habit has given birth to the borrowing habit. In the future, the borrowing habit may outgrow the spending habit and take you down.

If you start a saving habit, create an additional habit that can encourage you to keep saving. By learning to invest in the future, you could start enjoying the process of investing, and thus want more of it.

The problem with bad habits is when they start eating away your future. Because we have become 'the now generation', when times are tough right now, we look at whatever was set up for either future emergencies like insurance policies, or future investments and we want to cash them now. People borrow against their insurance policies or simply cash them to support an on-going dysfunctional habit

Some of us go to the equity in our houses and borrow against that, setting ourselves five years backwards from settling that mortgage bond, thus leaving ourselves bonded for life. Cashing your insurance policy, which was meant for the future, to cover immediate needs is to steal from your future self. Not investing your gratuity in growing investments is to steal from your future self. Borrowing money from the equity in your home is to steal from your future self. Cashing your investments into projects that are not going to multiply your money is stealing from your future self. The only advice is: stop stealing from your future self.

Does Money Slip Through Your Fingers?

There is a saying that money slips through your fingers. This only happens with habits that don't seem to be habits at all. A true habit doesn't seem odd at all. In fact, it is your default behaviour.

There are a lot of normal daily routines that consume money, but they are the least suspects when it comes to controls. You may think big items consume money, but it is actually consumed by daily routines that you don't think you need to examine at all. If you take lunch for example, If you habitually spend 30 bucks on lunch when you're at work, after a month, you shall have spend about 660 bucks, and after a year, that adds up to 7'920 bucks per year. This figure hardly goes into the budget but it is a habitual money consumer.

Other seemingly small things through which money may slip are such things as your cell phone. You may talk without the thought of the fact that it is costing you money, until the bill arrives. When you compute these bills over a year, you will see how much money you are consuming just through talk. Then you will know that talk is not cheap. Create some saving rituals:

- Open a savings bank account
- Sign a debit order for monthly deductions
- Habitually examine your statements to see what progress you are making
- Have a money day in each month, wherein you will look at everything to do with your money for that month. That allows you to make adjustments in the next month towards your great goals.

Chapter 8

8. Will You Pay Yourself First?

"A part of all you earn is yours to keep".
George Clason

Who gets paid first when money comes into your possession? Most people are used to paying everyone else but themselves. Their money follows urgency bells that ring incessantly. The bills are demanding and seem to be very urgent. If you paid attention only to the urgent, you will forget the important things. Yes a bill may sound urgent, but in order of importance, it is not more important than paying yourself first.

The only way you will pay yourself first is to make a contract with yourself. This contract is more important than any other contract that you have with anyone else. Every time money comes to you, regardless of the source, put aside at least 10% for yourself. This is not money to be spent on anything, but rather, money to be invested for growth. You can put this money in what Loral Langemeier, author of *The Millionaire Maker,* calls "the wealth account". It is not to stay in the bank forever, it needs to be invested in what I call "money trees". We'll look at these money trees when we look at the skill of investing.

Paying yourself first is the key to building wealth. It requires commitment on your part. It requires the strong will to reject the desire to spend money. It requires your focus on your money goals.

Many people say they want to get rich, but they find it hard or impossible to keep money. They remain uncomfortable in the presence of cash. When money comes, their instincts are to spend it.

Paying yourself does not include "spoiling yourself". Spoiling yourself is spending, not keeping money. The purpose of paying yourself is so that you have money to invest.

Goal based Savings

Your Cash Reserves

It has often been said that you need to have at least six months of your monthly income saved up. If you earn, for example, 10'000 bucks, you need to have at least 60'000 buck saved up.

The six months is based on the idea that, should you lose your current job, it could take you up to six months to get a new job. That figure must be adjusted in accordance with the amount of time it takes you to get a new job in your economy. This money will be used to pay your normal bills while you are in between jobs. This is not necessarily wealth-building money, but this is really your emergency money. Losing a job could be one of the biggest emergencies you may encounter in your life.

Saving for future expenses

Apart from your reserves, you may have other goals that you may want to save money for. These are in addition to your six months reserves.

It is a good idea to save money for future

expenses to avoid paying for them through debt. But remember that that is not equivalent to saving money to invest. You can save for holidays, car, furniture, gadgets, emergencies, or even education, but remember all of that money will be spent. That is not what we mean by paying yourself first.

Saving for investments

Saving for investments should be part of your overall savings strategy. You can set a goal to save for a deposit on your house. Even though some financial institutions do give a 100% mortgage, it is a great idea to have a deposit for your house, as well as extra money for closing costs when you buy your house. A deposit reduces the amount of money you have to borrow, and as a results, reduces your monthly instalment commitment, which will obviously be going on for a long time.

You can save for other investments such as lump sum investments with fund managers, or even to start your own business in the future. Saving for investments is like setting aside seed money that will be planted for growth in your investments.

Consider the Power of Compound Interest

Compound interest has been said to be the eighth wonder of the world. Compound interest benefits from time and patience. When you put money in an investment, you have to have the patience to let it grow. This speaks to long term investing. Start early. It is however, never too late wherever in life you are. The worst thing you can do is to delay.

Even though commercial banks have some investment products, what you really need to use is an investment bank. Most commercial banks focus on lending money out to their clients, while investment banks focus on investing money for their clients. You need to do your homework.

Action Plan

Because we human beings are creatures of

habit, I strongly suggest that you make a decision now to start new habits. The first new habit you should start grooving into your system is the habit of saving; regardless of how much debt you are in.

Most people might argue that they need to get out of debt first before they can start saving. But if it will take you five years to get out of debt, then you will never get started with your saving, and you are losing the power of compound interest working in your favour.

Building a personal ritual requires defining very precise behaviours and performing them at specific times. If saving is to be a habit, it must be performed regularly for a specific reason.

Save money by creating peculiar rituals:

- Save all the 10 bucks bills from your wallet at the end of each day.
- Bring your lunch to work every Monday, Wednesday, and Friday until the end of the year, or whichever days work for you.
- Boost your savings by 1% every time you get a raise.

- Save 10% of every bit of money that comes to you, from whatever source.

When you have savings, your lifestyle may be characterized by things you can actually afford, such as a house that won't get repossessed, a car that might not be repossessed; furniture that is in your name; and unbounded joy!

Save today – live safely tomorrow!

3rd Skill

INVESTMENTS

The Planting of Money Trees

Chapter 9

9. Investment Classes

"To make a lot of money, you will have to decide to become somewhat abnormal ... take on an abundance consciousness that is different from the way most people think."

Stuart Wilde

Think of an ant. It is always busy. It is not only busy with today's worries; it is working hard to ensure that there will be food in the burrows tomorrow. Ants have always survived great cataclysms because they invest in their future. A grasshopper on the other hand, will consume everything right here, without any thought for tomorrow.

According to Investopedia.com, an investment "is a monetary asset purchased with the idea that the asset will provide income in the future or appreciate and be sold at a higher price"

Investing is a key to success in life. Investing is about making sure that the future is as good as, or better than the past. A person, who does nothing today to ensure that the future is taken care of, is like a locust that gives no thought for the future, but consumes everything here and now.

In this section we will look at a few wealth building systems you can use to secure your future. I like referring to these as money trees. All things being equal, a fruit tree will give you its fruit every season in perpetuity. If you want future fruit, you have to plant these trees now. That is why I call investment systems money trees.

There are various investment vehicles one can use to make sure that the future is secure. Let us look at a few systems that can produce perpetual income for the investor. These systems include pension, real estate investments, the stock market, using investment funds, and of course business.

In this section we will start looking at pension or retirement annuity, and in subsequent chapters we will examine the other wealth-building systems.

Pension or Retirement Annuity

"Let not the young man of today steal from the old man to come"

In 1875, The American Express Company introduced one of the first retirement schemes in the industry. The wording of the scheme was: "a pension will be provided to worn-out or disabled employees who have been in employment for twenty years".

In 1875 a lot of jobs were labour intensive, and one could be "worn-out" within 20 years. Things may be different today in that people live longer. That therefore means that people have to save more for their retirement.

Let us take an example of three people contributing separately to their individual retirement funds. One contributes 500 bucks per month; the other contributes 1'000, while the third contributes 2'000. Let's say they each contribute for twenty years, that is, 240 months, and their money grows at an annual rate of 9%. Their future values are shown in the table below:

	Contribution	Time	Interest rate	Future Value
	RETIREMENT CONTRIBUTION			
A	500	20 years (240 months)	9%	333'943
B	1'000	20 years (240 months)	9%	667'887
C	2'000		9%	1'335'774

Table 1

The future value of 500 bucks contributed for 20 years, that is 240 monthly contributions will give you only three hundred and thirty three thousand, nine hundred and forty-three bucks (333,943); whereas 2'000 contributions will yield over 1,3 million as indicated in the table above.

Pension fund law allows you to take a third of this value as a lump sum without taxation, while the remaining two-thirds will be used to buy an annuity.

If we assume that each of our contributors will each receive a pension for a fixed period of 20 years, then we can calculate their monthly pension income as per the table below:

RETIREMENT ANNUITY					
	1/3 Lump Sum	Balance in the fund	Retirement period	Interest rate	Monthly Income
A	110'201	223'742	20 years (240 months)	5%	1'447
B	220'402	447'484	20 years (240 months)	5%	2'953
C	440'804	894'968	20 years (240 months	5%	5'906

Table 2

As can be seen, once the one-third lump sum is deducted from the future value, the remaining balance is used to purchase an annuity, which can only give you a monthly income of 1'477 bucks per month in the case of "A" above.

Comparing this with a person who contributed more, you can see in the table above that it is better to contribute more than to do the bare minimal.

Too many people let themselves do too little on their part and hope that fate will do the rest. Currently the inflation rate is too high, the lending interest rate too high, and the savings interest rate is too low.

The only friend of you money is time. You need time to grow your money. The power of compound interest is most effective when given ample time. Give your money ample time to grow. Start investing in your future now.

Now let's consider the scary part: How long after retirement, do you project that you will live? Another 20 to 30 years?

The truth is, in spite of new diseases coming up, due to advances in medical technology, people tend to live longer. All things being equal, as economists like to say, have you done enough towards your golden years?

Chapter 10

10. Real Estate

"Get four green houses and trade them up for one red hotel"
Monopoly

The board game of Monopoly is one of the best ways to teach yourself and your children about real estate. The theme that runs through the game is as stated above. After acquiring the lot, you buy up to four green houses every time it's your turn, and then you trade them up for one red hotel. Once you have the red hotel, you can make a whole lot more money than when you still had just houses.

Investing through Real Estate is one of the ways that people can "plant money trees". Even though rental income is a major part of real estate, as can be seen through the hotel business, making money through real estate goes beyond rental income.

If you have a piece of real estate that is being rented out, it can provide you with an income for as long as that piece of real estate is in demand and is habitable for its use.

There are various classes of real estate that we will discuss in this chapter. Before we go to the sectors, let us consider certain factors that are common to almost all sectors and sub sectors of real estate.

Cash Flow

In all sectors of real estate, you need to be aware of your cash flow. Your goal should always be positive cash flow.

In the book *The Money Field*, I spoke of 'the sponsoring rule', where a landlord is paying more to the bank in mortgage than the rent is covering; thus sponsoring a tenant to live in the landlord's property. This is an example of negative cash flow situation, which should be avoided by all real estate investors.

There are things that can be overlooked, but if they are, they may cost you lots of cash in the future.

For such things, you need to collect the cash upfront. Such things include future maintenance costs, administration fees, rates and taxes, and management fees. Your rental income needs to account for all these issues upfront. One more factor that needs to be considered is the vacancy factor.

The Vacancy Factor

In all sectors, you need to know the split between the occupancy rate and the vacancy rate in the short, the medium, and the long term.

By knowing the vacancy rates of your location and sector in advance and periodically, it gives you opportunity to price your property correctly.

When a building is vacant, it is obviously not collecting rent. However, the mortgage repayments don't stop. It is therefore important to include this vacancy rate in your rent, so that in the even that the building is without a tenant, there is money to continue paying the mortgage and other costs associated with owning the building.

How Do You Calculate Your Rent?

To avoid negative cash flow and the sponsoring rule, you need to include all of the following factors into your rental:

- Mortgage repayment (interest and capital)
- Administration fees (rent collections, bookkeeping, contracts and legal issues, etc.)
- Maintenance costs
- Rates and taxes
- The vacancy factor (as per your location)
- Your profit margin (this is a business, it needs to make a profit)

If these factors are not included when you calculate your rent, you are most probably running a negative cash flow business. That begs the question: why would you knowingly lose money?

Let us now look at the various sectors of real estate.

Chapter 11

11. Sectors of Real Estate

"Make of thy home a profitable dwelling"
George Clason

There are about six main sectors of real estate that we will discuss in this chapter. The distinguishing factors about each of these sectors are the clientele that they each serve. Each subsector also serves a different submarket. Legal issues are therefore different and the business models around each sector and subsector is different. The type of lease you will use in each sector is an important part of your business model. Let's look at each sector

1. Residential Sector

This sector of investments is vast and covers many subclasses. If you choose to invest in this sector you need to do a lot of homework so that you can choose which class or classes within this sector you would like to focus on. The residential sector is often classified in terms of population density or by construction costs or value. The three population density classes are: high density, medium density, and low density.

High density is where you will find low cost housing, medium density is where you will find medium cost housing, and low density is where you will find high cost housing.

The housing sector will further be classified into flats or apartments; townhouses; or traditional housing. These are found across the various densities.

Low cost housing will include low cost flats, low cost townhouses, and low cost traditional houses. Medium cost housing includes medium cost flats, medium cost townhouses, medium cost traditional houses. In the same way, high cost housing includes high cost flats, high cost townhouses, and high cost traditional houses.

You further get mixed developments within

each density class.

When you choose to invest in the residential sector, you need to make your choice clearly because each density class and cost level defines the economic character of your clients. This will therefore dictate the types of contracts you will be entering into for the sake of your business.

You will need to be aware that if you are operating in high-density areas where you are renting out low cost housing, you may be dealing with the unbanked, and thus you will have to be aware that your rent collection method may be cash based. Banking technologies that are cell phone based is obviously bridging this gab. This does not however, take away the inherent risks of this sub sector of the residential sector.

The medium density, medium cost sector caters mostly to the middle class.

If you want to operate in the low density, high cost sub sector, you need to be aware of all the risks inherent to this sub sector, which may include high vacancy rates, and high expected rentals. A prolonged vacancy of your property may affect your ability to service your mortgage, which may threaten your investment.

To fully understand this sub sector of real estate, and indeed all sector of residential real estate, you need to read and study and do your homework thoroughly. One of the books you might consider reading is Dolf de Roos' book, *Real Estate Riches.*

2. Commercial Sector

Commercial real estate refers to the office sector. Just like the residential sector, your location is vitally important when choosing where to invest. This will determine the economic character of the tenants you will attract. It is obvious that you are dealing with the business sector, and therefore your awareness of the economic conditions of not only your town or city, but also your country, and region is very important because those economic cycles will affect your business.

A high level of awareness allows you to be

active in making decisions that will be beneficial to your business at all times. Your flexibility in adjusting your rentals to each economic condition while keeping your eye on your cash flow will ensure your success. Your potential clients for this sector are all business sectors, the government and non-governmental organisations.

3. Industrial Sector

This sector includes warehousing and industrial space. Your clientele is mainly the manufacturing sector of the economy. Industrial spaces are in demand during a booming economy as well as a stable economy.

Warehousing and storage spaces are also in demand in an economy with a large retail sector. Supermarkets and apparel stores need spaces to store their stock.

If you want to participate in this sector of real estate, you need to be flexible and adaptable to economic shifts. This may often include readjusting your warehouse or industrial space for the next tenant if one should leave.

4. Retail Sector

This sector is mainly about shopping malls and shopping centres. To be a participant in the ownership of a mall or shopping centre often requires you joining with other investors. You may buy a sectional title to be part of a big mall or be a shareholder in a scheme or company that develops these centres. Your tenants are obviously big and small supermarkets as well as shops that surround these in a typical mall. One characteristic of a mall is its requirement for large parking spaces. While it is easy in the commercial sector to allocate numbered parking spaces to each tenant, in retail you need lots of space for employees, and customers to make the mall successful. Many malls now charge a minimal parking fee for customers of the mall, thus making sure that even the parking space makes some money.

5. Agricultural Sector

This is self-explanatory since it covers the vast of agricultural land, which range from crop production to animal husbandry.

To make money from agricultural land may include you being a farmer, or leasing your land to farmers. Crop farmers depend on the yield from the land and being able to sell their harvest. Animal husbandry is all about raising animals on the land and being able to sell them at a profit. However way you do it, make sure that you have a highly functional business plan and you follow a profitable business model.

6. Multi-use Real Estate

Very often, certain pieces of land have a combined use or are zoned for multiple purposes. You can have a mixed development residential area where flats, townhouses and houses are on the same lot or where commercial and retail share a piece of land, often with retail on the ground floor and commercial starting on the first floor going up.

You can participate in these schemes through sectional title ownership of various developments.

7. Raw or Undeveloped Land

This includes mostly undeveloped land. Speculating in undeveloped land requires a lot of money upfront that is not bearing much fruit in the beginning. There is no positive cash flow to speak of when you are not collecting any rentals or leasing fees.

Only when you know the future development plans of an area can you buy land that might be in demand in the future, hoping to cash in on capital gains.

All these sectors and their various classes function differently to each other. A person who is interested in Real Estate must carefully consider which area of real estate they want to go into, perform due diligence and understand all there is to understand about that sector and class of real estate.

Feasibility studies are very important before you go into real estate, mostly because of the high costs involved in this investment sector. If you are a Real Estate investor, you have to get comfortable with a lot of things that require your time and attention.

You can be:

- A buyer for rental or for resale
- A developer for rental or for resale
- A flipper, who buys and renovates old houses, either for rental or sale

Whatever you do, you must get comfortable with reading numbers. The most important financial word in real estate is: *positive cash flow!* This ensures that whatever transactions you do, they yield positive cash flow. Negative cash flow means you are losing money, while positive cash flow means you are making money. You must get a lot of advice.

Chapter 12

12. The Stock Market

"All great achievements are the result of a multiplicity of minds working together harmoniously"
Napoleon Hill

The stock market is another investment class that may require a certain level of technical ability. Investing on the stock market means "buying a share, or a portion" of a listed company.

When a company wants to expand its operations, it can "list on a stock exchange". This means they invite the public to give them money, in exchange for a stake in the company. You give them your money; they give you a share certificate.

There is a lot that can be said about this

investment class. If you are interested, there are a number of books that you can read to familiarise yourself with this topic. One website that can be very useful in teaching you a lot of things about investing, is www.investopedia.com. On this website, you can sign up for daily, weekly, or monthly newsletters that teach various things on finance. There are also tutorials and articles that you can search for depending on what topic you are trying to understand.

To get involved in the stock market, the first thing you need to do is to find a broker and open an account with them. Accredited brokers are often listed on the website of the stock exchange. Once your account is open you can start trading.

What to buy?

If you are a first time trader, your best bet is to buy blue chip companies. A blue chip company is defined by investopedia.com as *"A nationally recognized, well-established and financially sound company. Blue chips generally sell high-quality, widely accepted products and services."*

Investopedia.com furthers states: *"Blue chip companies are known to weather downturns and operate profitably in the face of adverse economic conditions, which helps to contribute to their long record of stable and reliable growth."*[3]

To buy blue chip companies listed on your local stock exchange, you can ask your broker to make some recommendations for you.

However, one of the ways to make your choice is to buy companies that you yourself know and support. Many of the businesses that you deal with may already be listed on your local stock exchange. Your bank may be a listed company; your grocery store where you shop regularly may already be listed on the stock exchange. Other companies from which you shop such as your clothing companies and restaurants may be listed on your stock exchange. This makes it easy for you to feel like "one of the

---

[3] The name "blue chip" came about because in the game of poker the blue chips have the highest value. Read further:
http://www.investopedia.com/terms/b/bluechip.asp#ixzz3jFMuwcOg

owners" each time you go into such a business.

How do you make money?

When you own a share of a company, when they make a profit and declare dividends, you get to benefit by being one of the beneficiaries who receive these dividends. This may happen quarterly, semi-annually, or annually, depending on when the companies that you hold declare dividends.

The second way to make money is to sell your shares on the secondary market to someone else, through the brokers of course. You make capital gains if the price you sell your share for is higher than the price you paid for it. You make a capital loss if the price you sell your share for is lower than the price you paid.

As you become more familiar with the stock market, you will discover more and learn to build a portfolio of shares.

How to build a portfolio

A balanced portfolio is one that contains companies in various sectors of the economy. You may want to distribute your portfolio by percentages in various sectors. Sectors often include:

• The banking sector, which will have all the listed banks.

• The financial services sector will include a lot of non-bank financial companies such as insurance companies and investment fund companies.

• The retail sector will include grocery stores and other apparel companies.

• The commodities sector or the mining sector will include all the listed mining companies and commodities companies such as oil and gas companies.

Depending on the size or your stock exchange, you will have various other sectors such as the real estate sector; the resources sector; the manufacturing sector; the services sector, etc.

A balanced portfolio will include these sectors in varying percentages. The reason you should have a balanced portfolio is to make sure that if one sector is economically adversely affected, the other sectors can balance out your portfolio.

The mining sector for example, may be affected

by strikes that may affect the production process. This may affect the price of shares on the stock market. It is for such time as these that the rest of the other sectors may help to support your portfolio.

There are quite a lot of things that go on at a stock exchange beyond trading of shares. There are bonds, exchange traded funds, indices, and many other tools that can be used in an investment strategy. Your Do It Yourself (DIY) experience will take you from the main board of a stock exchange to various other boards and products that are available, depending on your interest.

Investment Funds

Another way to grow your money is to use investment fund managers by purchasing financial instruments such as unit trusts, money market funds, offshore investment policies, and other tools used by investment managers.

This is another area that needs you to visit your financial advisor so that you can get more specific investment advice in this field. It is always a good idea to read as much as possible in any of these seemingly obscure investment systems before you are involved.

Many of these products are sold by investment banks, insurance companies, as well as commercial banks and fund management companies.

Chapter 13

13. Entrepreneurship

"Your greatest success and prosperity in business and life will come from your ability to create your own breakthroughs."
Jay Abraham

One of the biggest money trees is minding your own business. You can start your own from scratch, buy an existing business, or buy into a franchise. Entrepreneurial abilities are important when you go into business. A lot of books and articles have been written on the subject of entrepreneurship. Depending on the type of business that you want to go into, it is important that you start and function in an industry that you understand fully. The industry in which you have been or are currently employed may be the best place to start. Entrepreneurial skills are separate from industry knowledge. If you are trying to learn these skills at the same time that you are trying to learn the industry, you might be courting temporary failure. As an example, a teacher who has spent the majority of their life in the education sector, should probably not immediately start a business in the construction sector, about which he knows nothing.

They are better off starting their business in the education sector, because they have a vast knowledge about this sector. All they have to learn are entrepreneurial skills, but it can be assumed that they already know a lot about the sector. Once they have acquired entrepreneurial skills such as management, leadership, product development, marketing, and customer relations, etc., only then can they enter another sector where they only have to learn about the sector, and not necessarily entrepreneurship.

Some people reading this book may or may not be entrepreneurs yet, and may be looking for some pointers to get started. Here are a few pointers.

1. Financial Viability

Before you start any venture, you need to determine the financial viability of the idea. It is not good enough to have a brilliant idea if you can't monetize it. The purpose of a business is of course to create solutions for the world, but you must also be rewarded with profits for your work. Entrepreneurs are problem solvers who profit from the solutions they create.

Here are the important things about the finances of your enterprise:

- Even if you initially finance it by debt, the business must take over and finance itself.

- Yes it must be able to pay off the debt, and be able to support itself and its entire staff, including you.

- It must also be able to expand and grow itself. This means, out of its own profits, it must be able to grow its own markets and product lines.

- A business that is perpetually dependent on debt will eventually fold. Its creditors will one day take it over.

2. Personal Skills and abilities

These speak of your emotional body, your mental body, and of course your physical body. The latter speaks of your stamina and your ability to work hard and long hours. Your emotional body speaks of your reactionary body. How do you react to stress? Are you easily upset or do you have the emotional fortitude to remain calm when your emotions are stirred?

How do you respond under pressure? Do you give

in, throw a tantrum, or do you keep focused on the goal, doing your best to accomplish your mission. Do you take short cuts to "get rid" of the pressure, or do you keep doing the right thing? If you do your client wrong, you will lose that client eventually. You must understand yourself and know yourself so that you can keep working on your character to build a strong emotional body.

Your mental body speaks of your knowledge. Do you know enough about your enterprise to be able to solve problems easily? The more you know the easier it is to run the enterprise. Always work to increase your knowledge on your subject matter and related subjects. People who have great knowledge and great minds can solve problems easier, and reduce their stress levels on their emotional and physical body. Knowledge is power.

3. Management skills

Managing your enterprise is a function of a number of management skills that you need. At a personal level, you must be able to manage your time well. This means not wasting time on things that don't need your attention, and prioritising your time on productive things. Thus time management is a priority skill that you must master.

Can you keep track of your money? Money management is a major skill in entrepreneurial development. Your business is about making money, and therefore your ability to keep track of your money is key to your success.

Keeping track of your money means keeping good records. How much of your money is still in the hands of others, your debtors, and how long has it been there? When is it coming home?

How much of the money you have is actually not yours, and should be passed on to your creditors?

How much of the money that you make in your business do you actually keep, through investments?

If you don't have financial management skills, you might need to take a short course in this subject, so that you become a great entrepreneur. When your business grows you will hire bookkeepers and accountants to account for your money, but you still need to have an idea about your money.

4.   Setting up shop

Setting up shop is more than the physical setting up of your shop. It starts with the legal elements. Decide whether you are going to run as a sole trader or an incorporated entity. These two structures have different tax implications. As a sole trader you will be taxed as an individual, while a corporation gets taxed differently as a separate legal person.

It is a great idea to incorporate, that is, register a company that will have its own tax identification number. This will help you to un-comingle your personal life from that of your business.

Setting up includes opening bank accounts and setting up accounting books for your business. If some of your clients will be corporations and companies, find out what you need to do to register your business as a supplier on their databases. Most big companies keep a database of suppliers and only do business with businesses on their database.

Setting up shop also includes the physical space where you will function. If your business is starting in your home, create that separate space where you will run it. You don't want to be taking business calls while the television is loud and other members of the family are enjoying themselves watching TV. Create a separate space that can be respected as your business space. Set it up in such a way that even you are proud to call it your business.

5. Time is money, buy it back

If you are going to be working from home, the temptation to also become your own domestic worker will be there. Domestic work can be a lot of work that will steal your time away from your business.

It may seem like you are saving money, but it will work out cheaper to hire help than to try to do it yourself. Making a sales phone call that could bring in thousands of bucks into your business is better than doing laundry that brings nothing in terms of cash.

The fact is, you don't know which phone call will bring in the money, so you need to keep focused on your business and not get distracted.

6. Keep it flowing

The real secret of success in your business is to keep the work flowing. You need to be regular about working in your business as well as working on your business.

Working in your business means executing deals and selling products and services. Working on your business means improving your product line or your business processes. You can always hire people to work in your business, but only you can work on your business. Never stop innovating because you are too busy working in your business. Don't stop working when you feel swamped by work, rather increase your capacity to deliver, even if the increased work is seasonal. You can always hire temporary workers to help you in your season of plenty, and get back to "normal" thereafter. But you can work to make your abnormal times your new normal.

7. Customer is king

Customers, customers, customers! Henry Ford said it is not the employer who pays wages, but it is the customer. The employer is just the custodian of the money, but without customers, there will be no money to pay the bills.

There is no greater truth than that. Customers are the lifeblood of your business. Customers are the ones who will finance your life, your business, your growth, and everything about your business. The idea that customer is king goes beyond them being right in your marketing strategy, they are also right in your cash flow.

Create strategies for customer acquisition. The business guru, Jay Abraham says there's only three ways to grow your business. You must increase your customers, increase your product line, and increase the frequency of purchases by your existing clients. If you increase any of these areas by 10% each, your business will grow by over 33%

4th Skill

VALUE

Growth and Preservation of Resources

Chapter 14

14. Focus on Creating Value

"When tomorrow becomes today, will yesterday have been worth it? Today is tomorrow's yesterday, make it count!"

Letshwene

The idea of building value is at the core of the wealth building process. Wealth is measured in terms of value. How much value are you building through your efforts over time?

If you start working at the age of twenty five and retire at the age of sixty five, how much value shall you have build over that time? Your balance sheet is the measure of your net worth. But we all know that there are valuable things that you can build over time that do not appear on your balance sheet.

The value of your education and your relationships will obviously not appear on your balance sheet, even though they cost money.

Using your money and resources to build value is about asking the question: what is your money doing for you? And the next question is: what are you doing with your time.

Time and money are great partners in building value. For money to grow, it requires time. Time wasted is never regained.

Everyone can claim to not have enough money, but no one should claim that they have no time because everyone on our planet gets an equal amount per day. Everyone gets 24 hours per day. Yes we don't get an equal number of years, but we all get equal amount per day. Life should be lived one day at a time. Make this day count.

Building great value is not going to happen in one fell swoop! It happens in small increments, and it is to the increments that one should pay attention.

When you buy a house of great value, you pay your instalments one month at a time until the house is yours. To have great savings you need to save a little bit at a time, and allow time and compound interest to work for you. Don't procrastinate building great value in your life. It is the little efforts that you do today that will grow exponentially tomorrow.

Create a list of the most valuable things for you. Figure out how much time, money, effort, and other resources you need to commit to building these things of value.

When it comes to building wealth, you need to focus on wealth building systems of your choice. We have discussed these systems when we talked about Investments systems in previous chapters. Choose, focus and create.

What is the value of money in your hands?

Most of us understand that money is very valuable. But for most of us, we don't really see the intrinsic value of money, but only as a tool to get us things that are valuable.

If you don't see money as a valuable thing, you will not be interested in accumulating it. You will not be interested in preserving it, and you will not be interested in growing it. All you will want to do is spend it or send it to acquire for you the things that you think are valuable.

Include money among the things you value. Do not see it only as a separate necessary evil that can get you the things you want. If you place great value on money itself, you will not want to waste it. Value it on its own account. Let it feel your love for it. Build a relationship with money. Think about the idea of just having money. See what your attitude about the idea of having money is. If you place value on it, you don't have to have it only to do something with it. You can have it just because you value it.

Let us look at how we treat things that are valuable to us, and compare with our attitude towards money. People who value relationships would do whatever it takes to preserve those relationships. They will travel long distances to visit a friend or relative. They will do whatever it takes to mend a broken relationship.

People who value their property will do

whatever it takes to keep that property in tiptop condition. People who love their cars make sure that they are clean and serviced all the time. People who value their furniture make sure that there is not even a spec of dust on it and it is in good condition.

Why can't the money in your wallet enjoy the same privileges? Why can't you take out the bill in your wallet and make sure that it is not cruised and all bent up? Why can't you look at it with love and straighten its corners. Why is it sitting upside down in your wallet? Why can't you hold it in your hands and feel love for it? Just as you would hold your favourite item with affection, can you hold money with affection? Don't just fall in love with the "idea" of having lots of money, but with the cash itself, just as much as you love your car.

Money is one of the cornerstones of the human experience. The sooner you build a functional relationship with it, the sooner you can get on living your life to the full. Let us consider why we should build a separate, whole relationship with money. Let us face the facts that without money our lives will really be dysfunctional. Yes, it is a tool that enables us to get the things we want. But your car is also a tool that gets you from point A to point B and yet it enjoys your affection. Your furniture is also a tool upon which you rest when you are tired, and yet it enjoys your affection. Your clothes are also tools of comfort and decorum, and they enjoy your affection. Money is also a tool; it must also enjoy your affection, shouldn't it? All your other tools enjoy your care and affection, from your kitchen utensils to your lawn mower. They all get cared for. Besides, they were all acquired with your money. The cash in your wallet or bank account has a potential to be converted into more things that you like. I think it also deserves some love and attention. I think it is hypocritical to love the things that you acquire with your money but not to give money itself the same love and affection.

Think about that!

Chapter 15

15. Adopt The Farmer's Attitude

"Everyone can count the seeds in an apple, but only God can count the apples in a seed"
Robert H. Schuller

I like using the analogy of a farmer because a farmer has to rely on natural laws. They can't make up their own rules. They have to depend on the laws of nature and align themselves with natural processes.

A farmer has to have a seed to plant before he can even think of a harvest. He also has to plant in the right season at the right time and place. He needs to understand the conditions over which he functions. He needs to know, and not just guess what's going on. He can't just focus on the harvest. The planting is as important as harvesting.

Where does he start? He starts with a seed. The seed starts at the end of one harvesting season. When the harvesting season is over, he does not just think it's time to feast and eat the harvest. He intrinsically knows that he needs to preserve some of the harvest for next year or season's seeds.

There is an intricate link between the harvesting and the planting. There is no disconnection. One thing always leads to the other. The harvest leads to the planting and the planting leads to the harvesting and all the periods in between. There is no such thing as sitting around doing nothing.

No matter how little the farmer harvests, he always preserves seeds for the future. Even subsistence farmers intrinsically know this.

More often than not, a farmer will have labourers. They work in his fields. They don't own the land or the harvest. They just work for a wage.

Now, let's think about how a lot of us have our relationship with money constructed. We have a job that gives us a salary. We labour in the workplace for a salary. We don't own the workplace. We get a salary for our labour.

We should start to look at the salary as our own harvest. When the salary comes, what should we do? Should we consume the entire harvest? Is that what the farmer would do?

The farmer would preserve a seed for the next season. What if your relationship with money improved to where you are able to automatically think of some of your money as seed to be planted for the future? What if you started storing some of it in barns for the future, even for leaner periods that may be ahead? Saving and investing is a way of preserving your seed money for the future.

Why do the poor remain poor? Is it really poverty of resources or poverty of the mind or the thought process that goes into our relationship with money? Many people know they must save and invest money for the future. But most people see savings and investments as impractical. They are so focused on consumption that they feel they don't even have enough to consume. Consider what 'poor' subsistence farmers in the farming villages did to ensure that their future is always protected. After every harvest, they would set aside seed. To make sure that they don't even get tempted to consume this seed if times should be tough, they would soil this seed with ash. Once it is soiled this way, they have guaranteed their own survival by making sure that they will save this seed for next year's planting season. When tough times come, they would then be forced to consider other means of survival other than consuming the seed. During times of plenty, they would have ways of drying vegetables and preserving them for the winter season. Meat would be salted and preserved as well.

This is the level of survival. If you can't even guarantee your own survival, you are more dysfunctional than you have imagined, regardless of your "education" level.

What is Value?

Those who understand and possess the skill

called *value* are natural wealth builders. This skill gives you the ability to look beyond price. High price does not necessarily imply high value and low price does not necessarily imply low value.

When you read the book: *The Millionaire Next Door* by Dr Stanley & Danko, they write about the millionaires that they studied.

- These people do not even look like millionaires as defined by Hollywood
- They drive the old but very strong cars
- They live in the old but solid neighbourhoods
- When they buy something they make sure that it can last a long time (this ensures that they don't waste money buying the same thing over and over again)

When you have the skill called value:

1. You are not a wasteful person. People who waste resources end up wasting money because they have to buy the same thing over and over again, instead of just once. The money for the repeat purchase could be invested and growing.

2. You know how to preserve things and make them last longer. When you have the skill called

value, you know how to care for things. Yes, others may think you are stingy, but you are not. You give careful thought to everything that you buy.

3. When you have the skill called value, you are patient.

- Patience is very important in investments
- You understand the time value of money – that is, money, invested today needs time to grow
- You are willing to put your money away in projects that may take years to mature, but when they do mature, you will reap good benefits.
- Value does not mean you put your money away and forget about it, that is carelessness. You are aware and careful; but you are also patient.
- This is the patience of a farmer, who knows that all valuable things in life take time.

4. Value cannot be divorced from time! When you have value, you understand time. Value is build through time!

Wire Your Mind To See Value

1. Consider your buying habits. Do you focus on price or do you focus on the value of the things

you buy? Do you know what to look for in terms of value? Do you know what questions to ask your suppliers?

2.   Do you find yourself having to replace things before their allotted time is up? Was it carelessness on your part or was it the fault of the manufacturer? Before you blame the manufacturer, if you had exercised due care, could they have lasted longer?

3.   Do you have a home management system for household consumables?

4.   Do your groceries last as long as you had intended them to last? If they don't, was it a miscalculation on your part or was there wastage in the household?

5.   Many financial advisors might tell you to cut down on your spending. That might work, only if you cut down on wastage.

We talked about being "wired" right. In terms of the skill of value, what is your wiring like? Are you wired to waste or are you wired to preserve? Any wiring can only change once you're aware of it. These questions will help you to be aware of what your tendencies are. By installing the management systems necessary, you can, with time, change your wiring.

Most people will never be wealthy because they are wasteful. They waste resources. They waste money. They waste time.

Chapter 16

16. The Security Of Owning Your Home

"No man's family can fully enjoy life unless they do have a plot of ground wherein children can play in the clean earth and where the wife may raise not only blossoms but good rich herbs to feed the family."

George Clason

One of the most important indicators of value is when you own your own home. Owning your own home is such a basic thing that everyone needs to make it his or her primary focus.

To quote George Clason further:

"To a man's heart it brings gladness to eat the figs from his own trees and the grapes of his own vines. To own his own domicile and to have it a place he is proud to care for puts

confidence in his heart and greater effort behind all his endeavours. Therefore, do I recommend that every man own the roof that shelters him and his"

Financial institutions are indeed eager to lend money to people to start the journey of owning their own homes. You should however not get stuck on this journey. The fact that your mortgage company wants you to take twenty to thirty years to pay off your home does not mean you can't pay it faster, especially your primary home. A million bucks house paid over thirty years at the interest rate of 12% will cost you over 3.7 million bucks.

Let us compare this with your ability to pay off a very expensive car over only five years. A million bucks vehicle, paid over five years at the interest rate of 12% will cost you 1.3 million bucks

The prices of some of the most expensive cars exceed the prices of many average homes, and yet these cars get paid off in five years while you would take thirty years to pay off a home. Over a span of thirty years, people who change cars every five years will have bought six cars whose individual prices may exceed the value of your home. If one can pay off a car this fast, surely one can put the same focus on owning your first home.

Why Should You Own Your Home?

- A home provides security for you and your family
- Continually paying rent is equal to paying someone else's mortgage
- Economies are not stable, if your house is paid off, you don't have to worry that much during a bad year, and yet if it's not paid off, you worry the most during a bad year because you might just lose it. If you should lose your job during a bad economy, if your house is not paid off, you could lose it just like that.
- Owning your primary home fast gives you the freedom to invest in others things without fear.

Your House Is Not An ATM

One of the most elusive things about owning a house is the idea of equity. You buy a house for half a million bucks, you pay off half of it, and after a few years a property value estimator comes and tells you that your house is worth a million bucks. Don't confuse value with cash. If you do, you will think that you can start withdrawing that cash. This is what leads to equity loans. By taking a loan against your house, you are going further into debt, not getting out. Debt consolidation is not debt elimination.

• Don't take loans against your house to pay less valuable things like personal loans, credit cards, or even to buy cars. This is tantamount to extending the debts on those other items.

• Don't take loans against your house for risky business ventures. If these ventures fail, it is your house that will be repossessed.

For more understanding of debt management tools, please read *The Money Field*. In that book, I have devoted the third section to tools of credit and debt management systems.

5th Skill

CONTROL

The Power of Discipline – Within and Without

Chapter 17

17. What Is Control?

"Concentrate on what you know or on what works. Don't allow the lure of activity to take you beyond what is confortable and controllable"
Stuart Wilde

Control is a very important skill in the money game. The idea called discipline is essentially your ability to practice the skill of control. People may associate the word discipline with pain, only because it calls you to give up something - disempowering habits, in order to install new habits in your life.

People don't like giving up anything, especially habits. But if these habits are essentially your "wrong wiring", continually producing undesirable results, would you not give them up if you know exactly what to replace them with? Nature does not allow a vacuum. If you stopped bad habits, but you didn't replace them with good habits, you are very likely to gravitate back to your old habits. New habits will only take root if they are consciously repeated until they are your second nature.

Let us look at two ways in which we can exercise control in our finances: Physical control and Emotional control

Physical Control

Physical control in the money game talks about the structures you have in place to run your money game. One of the biggest problems people have in their money game is lack of structures. Money comes into a void and disappears without the owner really knowing what happened.

A subject that was meant to teach physical control is accounting. Accounting leads to accountability. We are not asking you take a course in accounting, although if you are in business you most probably should. But at home, it takes creating systems that help you to track your money. There are already systems in place that can help you

• Every time you spend money, you get given a receipt. That receipt is a trace for your money.

• The most basic level of financial controls start with the paper trail – if you kept all those receipts, you will know where your money went at any given time.

• That information can help you to make new decisions or give your money new direction if you don't like where it's been going

• You need to set up physical control systems that can help you to track you money – you don't have to be an accountant to do that.

• Have a "money day" each month. This is the day on which you take out all your receipts and all the papers associated with your money, and you have the money conversation with yourself. On this day, you will see where all your money goes. If you like where it goes to, you can continue with your current system. If you don't like the report you are reading about yourself, this is your opportunity to change. Change is in your hands. The money day gives you the right kind of data that you can use to make decisions. Without this data, you will always be groping in the dark.

Emotional Control

Emotional control speaks of your emotions and their relationship with your money. There are two basic emotions when we deal with money

- The Presence of Money feeling; and
- The Absence of Money feeling.

Which of these feelings are stronger?

What do you do in the *Presence* of money?

- Some people are afraid and uncomfortable in the presence of money – so they run and spend the money quickly.

- Some people are so excited that they can't contain the emotions – so they go and spend the money out of excitement.

- Some people are calm, calculative, methodical and logical. They tend to do "the right thing" with their money.

What do you do in the *Absence* of money?

- Some people *panic* when they have no money. Panic takes away rational thinking. They may end up doing things that they will regret. It is hard to give counsel to a panic stricken person.

- Some people get depressed – so much that they may self-destruct. They get into more irrational debt. They spend even more of what they do not have – on credit.

- Some people are calm, calculative, methodical and logical.

The goal is to always remain calm so that you can think clearly. Whether in the presence or in the absence of cash, you need to remain calm. The absence of money is not the end of the world. And the presence of money is not the end or the beginning of the world either.

Emotional control means the ability to be in charge of your faculties regardless of what conditions you find yourself in.

6th Skill

PROTECTION

Protecting your Wealth and Dealing with Vulnerabilities

Chapter 18

18. What Is Risk?

"All of human unhappiness comes from one single thing: not knowing how to remain at rest in a room"

Blaise Pascal

Feeling safe is a key ingredient in creating security. Every person has certain potential risks that need to be assessed, understood, and mitigated against. Risk assessment starts with answering a number of "What if ..." questions.

- What if I were to lose my income as a result of
    - Disease
    - Disability
    - Retrenchment
    - Retirement
- What if I were to lose my property as a result of
    - Fire
    - Theft
    - Damage

- What if I, or someone close to me were to get sick?
- What if someone should die and there is money needed for funeral expenses?
- What if I were to be sued for something I did or did not do?

All these questions, and more, are very important before a person can put a protection strategy in place.

The function of insurance is to help you to mitigate your risks. Almost all risks can be mitigated against through the use of insurance. Risk almost always has to do with potential loss.

The subject of protection may go beyond the traditional meaning of risk. There are other things in life for which you cannot buy insurance, but you may still suffer loss as a result of the structures that you are using.

If we take a structural system like marriage, a person may lose half of their possessions due to divorce while another may keep all their possessions even if they went through divorce. This has to do with how the marriage institution is set up. You can't take insurance to protect yourself against the risk of divorce, but being protected means setting up your systems in such a way that you minimize or eliminate potential loss. Sometimes people may make decisions that will lead to loss simply because they're ill advised or following untested strategies.

Business structures may also protect one person from paying too much tax, while another person, with certain systems, may end up paying more than they could have, if their systems were set up differently.

A person, who has a will and has done proper estate planning, can protect much more of their wealth even from beyond the grave, than a person who has not done any estate planning.

Mitigating risk is the first step in protecting yourself. In the next chapter, let us look at insurance products and how they can help us to mitigate risk, and also look at other legal entities that are used to protect wealth.

Chapter 19

19. Life insurance And You

"The happiness of those who want to be popular depends on others; the happiness of those who seek pleasure fluctuates with moods outside their control; but the happiness of the wise grows out of their own free acts"

Marcus Aurelius

No matter how diligently you build your financial empire, failure to purchase sufficient insurance can put you in a desperate hole in a heartbeat! You hope you never need it, but when the time comes, you're glad it's there.

When you buy a car, you make sure it is insured before you even drive it out of the shop floor, in fact, the bank won't let you drive off unless your …err I mean, … *their* asset is insured. Why? Because common sense tells you that failure to insure it may put you in an anxious position within a blink of an eye! Some reckless driver may change your plans in a flash!

We protect what we value the most: the car, the house and house contents. I now would like to make a case for personal insurance. Isn't it funny how we may insure all these material things, but forget the most important element: The owner! All your possessions are insured, but are you insured?

If your car gets involved in an accident, you can replace it if it is insured. Should a thief break into your house and steal your possessions, - you can replace them, if they're insured.

Well, what about you? If you are involved in some accident, can you afford to get yourself repaired? (Hospital costs). What if you are a write-off? - I mean you can't continue to do the things you used to do before. You are a "write-off" at your work. Redundant. No longer needed! Will you have enough money to continue living?

This is where *personal insurance* comes in! Now let's be frank. Many people never bother about making provision for their future, and end up regretting it. You think, when I get a better salary, I will start a savings account. You know what? Better salaries never come! Back to the issue at hand: what must I protect myself against? What are the risks?

The collective name for life insurance, disability cover and trauma cover is *"risk cover"*. Risk cover means protecting yourself against the risks in life. You therefore insure yourself against anything that could happen to you. This includes *disability, accidents, traumas such as illness, and even death.*

With *life insurance* you protect yourself and your family against the risk of dying suddenly. Life insurance is an agreement between you (the insured) and an insurer.

Under the terms of a life insurance contract, the insurer promises to pay a certain sum to someone (a beneficiary) when you die, in exchange for your premium payments.

Why would you need life insurance?

The most common reason for buying life insurance is to replace the income lost when you die. By buying life insurance, you are providing your beneficiaries with a *financial person* who will be there to continue to do what you used to do, at least financially, when you are no longer there.

Secondly, another common use of life insurance proceeds is to pay off any debts you leave behind to avoid causing financial problems for your family. For example, mortgages, car loans, medical bills, and credit card debts are often left unpaid when someone dies. These obligations must be paid from the assets left behind. This can deplete the resources that your family needs. Life insurance can be used to pay off these debts, leaving your other assets intact for your family to use.

Thirdly, Life insurance provides liquidity to your estate. That is, it provides cash. If you were to die now, would it be possible for the estate duty to be paid? You may leave some liquid assets (such as cash, and savings bonds), and some illiquid assets (such as real estate, a car, and maybe shares). Your liquid assets may not be enough to pay all the debts that you leave behind, plus all the expenses that arise because of your death (such as funeral expenses and estate taxes). Your illiquid assets may have to be sold in order to meet these obligations when they come due. This may cause a financial loss if the assets must be sold cheaply in order to get the money on time. Life insurance can avert this situation, because the proceeds are available almost immediately upon your death.

Fourthly, Life insurance creates an estate for your heirs. After your debts and expenses are paid, there may not be much left over for your family. Life insurance can automatically provide assets for them after your death.

Fifth, Life insurance can be a critical component for specialized business applications, such as funding a buy-sell agreement. Under a buy-sell agreement, life insurance can be used to provide cash for the purchase of a deceased owner's interest in the business. People in partnerships can take life insurance on each other's lives so that they can buy their partner out without having to dissolve the business.

Sixth, Life insurance may also be a great way to give to charity when you die. You may have always had a great philanthropic desire, but not the means to make it a reality. Life insurance can do that for you.

Finally, life insurance can be an investment vehicle. Some types of life insurance policies may actually make money for you, as well as provide the benefits described above. Most universal policies have an investment portion attached to them. This can help you with long- term financial goals.

What determines your life insurance need?

Your life insurance needs change as your life changes. When you are young, you may not have a need for life insurance, especially if you have no dependents. However, as you take on more responsibilities and your family grows, your life insurance needs increase. You should periodically review your needs in order to ensure that your life insurance coverage adequately reflects your life situation.

How much cover should I take?

There are several simple methods that you can use to estimate your life insurance need. These calculations are sometimes referred to as "rules of thumb" and can be used as a basis for your discussions with your insurance professional. Most insurance companies have such calculators on their websites.

Other Insurance Products

Insurance comes in handy when you especially have something to protect. Insurance helps to reduce the cost of replacement of your valuables. It is more cost effective to pay low premiums than to have to come up with the whole amount of replacing something valuable, should the need arise in case of loss.

Homeowner's insurance:

A home is a high value item in anyone's balance sheet. Fire, however, can destroy it within minutes. If it is insured against such a risk, it can be rebuilt within a few months with the insurance money.

The same can be said of other valuables such as vehicles, furniture, and businesses.

We face such risks as theft, damage, accidents, etc. that happen without warning. Insurance helps to mitigate against such risks.

Legal Entities

A natural person and a legal person are treated differently under the law under certain circumstances. Take taxes, for example. A natural person gets taxed right off the top from their gross earnings, while a legal person, like a company, gets taxed at the bottom, from its net profit.

Legal entities are tools used by the wealthy to protect their wealth. In her book, *The Millionaire Maker*, Loral Langemeier states the importance of legal entities as:

1. Creating liability protection
2. Ensuring asset protection
3. Keeping wealth accelerating through multiple streams of income
4. Optimizing opportunities, and
5. Maximizing tax strategies

Always seek advice as to which structures you should use. They are not all the same. Sole traders, corporations, partnerships, trusts, non-profit societies, non-governmental organisations; all have different implications with regards to your protection and tax implications.

7th *Skill*

SHARING

The Key to Abundance

Chapter 20

20. To Give Or Not To Give

"Wealth that is shared creates more wealth, and you can share many forms of wealth besides money"
Napoleon Hill

"Giving and receiving are different aspects of the flow of energy in the universe; ... and in our willingness to give that which we seek, we keep the abundance of the universe circulating in our lives"

Deepak Chopra

Giving and sharing is very important in all of our lives. Our willingness to share our blessings with others, allows them to experience the goodness we experience; and as we receive their gratitude, we feel more encouraged. It takes a healthy personality to view giving and sharing in its proper way. There are a few principles to follow when you give:

Principles Of Giving

• **Don't give to induce indebtedness or reciprocity**

o When you give to someone, just so that they will "owe you one", you are only giving to induce indebtedness. That means you will be waiting in expectation for them to "repay" the favour. That is not giving but sowing seeds of potential disappointments. In the event that they do not "repay" or return the favour, you will be disappointed. By definition, therefore, you were not giving freely.

• **Never give from a sense of duty or obligation**

• When you give only because it's your duty to do so, or you feel obligated to do, you will be creating a burden for yourself. This kind of giving is heavy and not sustainable at all. At the spiritual level, the recipients might not enjoy your gifts at all

- **Give cheerfully**
  - Giving cheerfully means you give without expecting anything in return. You give because you really want to help with all your heart.

- **Plan your giving**
  - Don't give haphazardly. Put your giving in your budget. Decide how much of your money will be dedicated to gifts. These may be gifts to family members because of birthdays, celebrations, or just your desire to help them out.
  - Don't exceed your planned giving by going into your own savings, or worse, by going into debt for someone else. When you take your planned savings and diverting them to gifts, you are stealing from yourself. When you go into debt so that you can give, you are cheating yourself.

Chapter 21

21. Lending And Borrowing Rules

"Neither a lender nor a borrower be."
William Shakespeare

Family members and friends, often "help" each other out through loans. It is important to lay out a few lending and borrowing rules.

Why Do People Want To Borrow Money From You?

Have you ever wondered why people want to borrow money from you? Are they just taking chances or have they read some signals from you? What are some signals that they may be seeing? They may see the car you drive that says I can afford this; or they may see the house you live in and the luxurious or comfortable furniture and lifestyle you lead. They may see your business and suspect that it's profitable; or they may have heard that your employer pays well, or that you just got an increase in your pay.

Every coin does have two sides, and here is the side they may not see about you: They may not know that your car is financed by debt; they may not know that there is a heavy mortgage on your house; they may not know that your furniture was bought on a hire-purchase contract and should you falter, it may all go under the hammer. They may not be aware of the line of credit that is sustaining your business. And about your generous employer, they may not even know what salary band you are on, or what other commitments you face.

When someone wants to borrow money from you, you have an opportunity to either sustain their perception about you, or give them a new perspective. Lending and borrowing among friends and family creates a new dynamic, which, if not handled well, could destroy the harmony that existed before.

Therefore, let there be a frank conversation and not a hasty action. The conversation should include frank points from both sides. If you know you cannot lend them money at all, for whatever reason, don't even go to the extent of asking how much they intend to borrow, because that creates an expectation. Declare your position immediately, and start helping them to explore alternatives. Don't forget, almost no one asks for money without a story; and most stories are meant to arouse your compassion. If you get lost in their story, you might lose your logic and get sucked in emotionally, which might lead to a quick decision to help, which might be regretted later.

If you think you can lend them some money, you can take the conversation to the next level. Without saying how much you have or how much they think they need, let the discussion move to the purpose of the loan. By discussing the purpose first, you might help them to find a solution that does not need any money, or perhaps not as much as they thought they needed.

Once you've agreed on the amount, do not skip the terms and conditions, regardless of how awkward or uncomfortable this step may be. It is the absence of terms and conditions that often complicate your demand for your money in the future, which compromises the relationship. Discuss the repayment plan and agree on it. Let there be a witness in the form of a common friend or another family member. Let it be in writing, with witnesses signing. Even without legal language, let it be clear how much is at stake, the time involved and the repayment process, whether in instalments or lump sum, and the costs involved, even if it's just the bank charges without you charging interest. All this can be done with a light heart and in the midst of laugher. (There might not be much laughter if these terms are broken).

Transfer the money through Internet banking or through the bank; or write a cheque; or deposit directly into their account to create some paper trail. Avoid handing over cash, especially without a witness. If you have to hand over cash, get them to sign acknowledgement of receipt, and keep the papers involved in that transactions. Let the witness also sign.

Don't lend more than you can afford to lose. Don't borrow more than you can afford to repay. Communicate any delays in the process. Respect your relationship and don't jeopardise it because of the loan.

- Never lend to solve a "problem"; you may be creating yet another problem in the form of debt. Don't borrow to solve a "problem".
- Never lend to friends & relatives unless you are prepared to forfeit. Don't borrow from friends & family, but you can let them invest in viable projects
- Don't lend what you are not prepared to lose
- Don't lend to whoever does not have a repayment plan
- Protect your relationships
- Have a repayment plan before you borrow
- Don't borrow unless you really, really have to … wait a day …

EPILOGUE

The Seven Essential Money Skills in a nutshell:

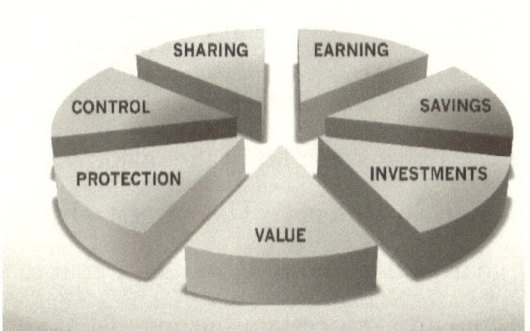

The above picture represents a slide that I have presented to thousands of people in the Money Skills workshop. The long and short of this book comes to these *Seven Essential Money Skills*.

Going clockwise, beginning with Earning:

The ability to *earn* money is the key to the money game. Unfortunately many people limit their earning capabilities by committing to sell only one skill or one talent, out of the many natural talents that they may have. To fully explore your earning capabilities, make a list of all your skills and talents and start employing all other skills and talents that remain unemployed. Lazy skills and lazy talents don't bring money in, but employed skills and talents will increase your income.

Saving Money is one thing that almost everyone has heard about, and yet it remains one of the hardest skills to acquire and implement. In the book *The Money Field*, I give you a list of the major reasons why people can't save money. The biggest obstacles are lack of goals and purpose. If you set a goal to save a certain amount for a certain purpose, what you need next is the strong will and discipline as well as the focus to achieve your goals!

Investing allows you to employ certain wealth building *strategies* with the money you have saved. By understanding these systems, it strengthens your resolve to save and invest.

In the final analysis, you need to be focused on building *value*. By focusing on performing assets throughout your working life, you will be able to look back at the value you have built over time. Building value is not an overnight thing; it is a commitment over time.

You can only *protect* what you have. As you save, invest, and build value, you need to think about protecting what you have. Insurance is one tool that you can use to protect yourself, as well as certain legal structures that you need to set up.

Control continues throughout your money game as both an internal and external battle. You need to tame and control your emotions so that they follow your mind, and you need to tame and control your mind to set up structures that will help you to win the game.

We do what we do because we would like to *share* it with those we love. Sharing must be done skilfully so that it does not end up destroying the entire tree from which we expect to reap more fruit next season. Share the fruit, not the tree.

I hope you have enjoyed this journey!

Thank you!

BIBLIOGRAPHY

1. Abraham, Jay. *Getting everything you can out of all you've got*, Piatkus, 2000

2. Bay, Tom. *Look Within or Do Without*, Career Press, 2000

3. Clason, George S. *The Richest man in Babylon*, Signet, 1988

4. De Roos, Dolf, *Real Estate Riches – how to become rich using your banker's money*, Warner Business Books, 2001

5. Gibran, Kahlil, *The Prophet*, Alfred A Knopf, 1923

6. Graham, Benjamin. *The Intelligent Investor*, revised edition, Harper, 2006

7. Hansen, Mark Victor and Allen, Robert G, *The One Minute Millionaire – the enlightened way to wealth*, Harmoney Books, 2002

8. Hill, Napoleon, *Think and Grow Rich*, Random House, 1960

9. Hill, Napoleon. *Grow Rich with Peace of Mind*, Penguin Books, 2007

10. Knight, JZ, *Ramtha, The White Book*, JZK Inc., 2004

11. Langemeier, Loral. *The Millionaire Maker*, McGraw Hill, 2006

12. Letshwene, R. Nelson, *Functional Mastery Over My*

Finances, Reach Publishers, 2008

13. Letshwene, R. Nelson. *The Money Field*, Moedi Publishing, 2015

14. Lunt Peter, and Livingstone Sonia. *Journal of Economic Psychology*

15. Patel, Raj, *The Value of Nothing – how to reshape market society and redefine democracy*, Portobello Books, 2009

16. Stanley, Thomas, J and William D. Danko, *The Millionaire Next Door*, Gallery Books, 1998

17. Swart, Nico, *Personal Financial Management*, 2nd ed, Juta, 2002

18. Wattles, Wallace, D. *The science of getting rich*, Thrifty Books, 2009

19. Wilde, Stuart. *The Trick to Money Is Having Some*, Hay House, 1998

20. www.investopedia.com

ACKNOWLEDGEMENTS

A teacher of mine once said, creativity is forgetting your source. What he meant was that you may sound creative, but you are only creative because someone else inspired you, even though you may forget who that is.

The inspiration for this book was a very small paragraph in a book by Robert Allen called One Minute Millionaire. He mentioned the seven essential money skills in passing. I spent many years contemplating those skills and building a presentation that has been heard by thousands of people in Botswana and South Africa. From their comments and questions, that presentation grew into this book. I have read and written many other articles that continued to add to the body of this book.

I am however grateful for my colleagues at the office who continued to give that presentation a chance. Oteng Orakanye (aka OT) continued to call many schools to afford the teachers a chance to listen to a presentation called The Seven Essential Money Skills. Thanks OT for your hard work! I am also grateful to Poloko Mongatane who learnt that presentation and continues to give it to many people across Botswana.

I am grateful for companies like Letshego Financial Services (Pty) Ltd and BancABC that sponsored some of the presentations to the many audiences we have reached.

We now have a book that will be able to cover a whole lot more information than the presentation has been able to cover, and participants can now take this home with them.

I am also grateful for the editors of newspapers like The Botswana Guardian and The Patriot on Sunday, where a version of some of these ideas were given publicity through the columns that I wrote for these papers.

Thank you to you the reader, for your interest in these concepts. I hope they have enriched your life as much as they have enriched mine.

ABOUT THE AUTHOR

Nelson Letshwene is a professional speaker and writer with over two decades of experience. For over 11 years he wrote a weekly column in *The Botswana Guardian*, The Silver-Line, which focused on financial literacy, financial planning, business, and personal development. The column has received great reviews from its readers throughout Botswana since its inception in 2002. He has also written for other newspapers and magazines including *The Patriot on Sunday*, and BG Investor Magazine, which is now renamed *Botswana Investor*. For over four years he has broadcasted his *Money Skills* talk show on radio to thousands of listeners.

He holds a Bachelor of Commerce degree from the University of the Witwatersrand (WITS), and an Honours Bachelor of Commerce degree from the

University of South Africa (UNISA), as well as several business certificates from The Insurance Institute of South Africa (IISA)

He is the author of numerous books and programs in the field of personal finance, motivation, and spirituality including *The Money Field*; *Your Longing is Your Calling*; and *Faith & Purpose*. These books are available on amazon.com in paperback as well as in digital format on amazon's kindle platform.

He is also a personal finance blogger: www.7moneyskills.wordpress.com

For more you can visit his website at www.nelsonletshwene.com

OTHER BOOKS BY R.NELSON LETSHWENE

Your Longing Is Your Calling (Moedi publishing house, 2011)

Your Longing is Your Calling is based on the Seven Desires of man. These are the deepest longings that each person needs in their lives. They go beyond the day-to-day needs even though the day-to-day needs are based on these. They are Love, Joy, Peace, Fulfilment, Health, Self-expression, and Prosperity. This book covers these seven topics in seven essays.

The Money Field – *In the game of money everyone is player, but some are more skilled than others.* (Moedi Publishing, 2015)

This book covers the money game on the Money Field. It covers all the rules applied in the game of money. It introduces you to other players on the field, and goes on to teach you how to grow your money, and how to handle debt, otherwise called other people's money.

Faith and Purpose – *Living your life to the full without fear, guilt, or regrets.*

This book covers the art and the science of the subject of faith. Faith is the art of becoming one of your desires and bringing them into reality. Purpose is faith with passion and direction. This book gives you the steps to building your faith and implementing it in your life.

Personal Financial Mastery – The Essential life skill seminar (An Audio program) (Moedi Publishing House – Botswana)

Mastery Over Debt (An Audio program) (Moedi Learning Technologies)

Other Electronic Books (eBooks) Include:

- The Retirement Report – What you need to know to build your nest egg. (Moedi Learning Technologies)
- Success is a Personal Thing – Join the money conversation
- Life Insurance and You

Other articles are published on: www.nelsonletshwene.com

For more information or to book a workshop, please call +267.390.5335 or email info@moedi.net

www.ingramcontent.com/pod-product-compliance
Lightning Source LLC
Chambersburg PA
CBHW031051180526
45163CB00002BA/777